Teaching English to Young Learners

Helen Emery and Sarah Rich

English
Language
Teacher
Development
Series

Thomas S. C. Farrell,
Series Editor

tesol
international
association

Typeset by Capitol Communications, LLC, Crofton, Maryland USA
and printed by Gasch Printing, LLC, Odenton, Maryland USA

TESOL Press
TESOL International Association
1925 Ballenger Avenue
Alexandria, Virginia 22314 USA

Senior Manager, Publications: Myrna Jacobs
Cover Design: Tomiko Breland
Copyeditor: Tomiko Breland

TESOL Book Publications Committee
John I. Liontas, Chair
Robyn L. Brinks Lockwood, Co-chair   Guofang Li
Margo DelliCarpini   Gilda Martinez-Alba
Deoksoon Kim   Adrian J. Wurr
Ilka Kostka

Reviewer: Deoksoon Kim

00057924

ISBN 9781942223450

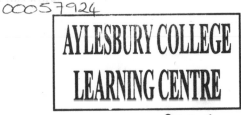

Contents

About the Authors

Dr. Helen Emery is an Associate Professor in the department of Curriculum and Instruction at Sultan Qaboos University, Oman. She has taught English and lectured in Applied Linguistics and Education in Africa, the Far East, Middle East and the UK for over 30 years. She is specifically interested in teachers' professional development and the teaching of early literacy.

Dr. Sarah Rich holds an honorary fellow position at the University of Exeter in the UK where she ran teacher education programmes for many years. She is currently an educational advisor on in-service teacher training for the Ministry of Education in the Sultanate of Oman. Recent publications include an edited volume entitled *International Perspectives on Teaching English to Young Learners*

Series Editor's Preface

The English Language Teacher Development (ELTD) Series consists of a set of short resource books for English language teachers that are written in a jargon-free and accessible manner for all types of teachers of English (native and nonnative speakers of English, experienced and novice teachers). The ELTD series is designed to offer teachers a theory-to-practice approach to English language teaching, and each book offers a wide variety of practical teaching approaches and methods for the topic at hand. Each book also offers opportunities for teachers to interact with the materials presented. The books can be used in preservice settings or in in-service courses and can also be used by individuals looking for ways to refresh their practice.

Helen Emery's and Sarah Rich's book *Teaching English to Young Learners* explores different approaches to teaching English to young learners and the various challenges this may present to a language teacher. Helen and Sarah provide a comprehensive overview of how to plan and teach English to young learners in an easy-to-follow guide that language teachers will find very practical for their own contexts. Topics on young learners include developing principles, understanding task-based learning, and literacy-related tasks. *Teaching English to Young Learners* is a valuable addition to the literature in our profession.

I am very grateful to the authors who contributed to the ELTD Series for sharing their knowledge and expertise with other TESOL professionals, because they have done so willingly without any compensation to make these short books affordable to all language teachers throughout the world. It is truly an honor for me to work with each of these authors as they selflessly gave up their valuable time for the advancement of TESOL.

Thomas S. C. Farrell

1

Introduction

In the last 15 years, the teaching of English as an additional language to young learners (hereafter referred to as TEYL) has expanded rapidly with huge numbers of younger and younger children worldwide receiving formal English language instruction. Not so long ago, TEYL was mainly concentrated on children between 9 to about 13 years of age. But today, the term "young learner" is widely applied to describe children learning English from the age of 3 all the way up to 14 years of age (Pinter, 2006).

Naturally, as TEYL continues to grow, the numbers of teachers working with young learners is also growing, particularly where English is taught as a foreign language. In our experience, homeroom teachers, teachers making the shift from secondary to primary teaching, and those starting their careers as young learner English language educators are quick to recognise that while teaching English to young learners can be a rewarding experience, it can also feel like a daunting task.

The purpose of this book is to introduce some guiding principles for TEYL and to show how these can be used to help teachers develop classroom practices that are both enjoyable and beneficial for the groups of young learners they work with. Our focus will be on working with young learners from first grade to Grade 6 (or children from 5–12 years of age) as this is the area of TEYL that has seen most rapid expansion in recent years. However, the principled reflective approach to TEYL we introduce here can also be adopted in the teaching of preschool children and older young learners in the lower reaches of secondary schooling.

In Chapter 2, we will consider insights from a number of key theoretical perspectives regarding children's language learning and the role of teachers in supporting this, which can help lay the foundations for effective TEYL practice. In the next three chapters, we will consider the ways in which these principles can be activated in classroom teaching.

In Chapter 3, we introduce task-based learning as a classroom approach that is ideally suited to helping young learners develop their knowledge and skills in English. Chapter 4 considers how we can implement task-based learning in the classroom and provides examples of the different sorts of tasks and activities that we can use to help learners develop fluency and accuracy in the target language. In Chapter 5, we turn to the importance of literacy development with young learners and investigate some tasks and activities that could help develop good reading and writing skills.

Finally, in Chapter 6, we discuss the role of reflective teaching in ensuring a good fit between the ideas we introduce in this book and teachers' own learners and teaching settings.

2

Developing Principles

Principles are the fundamental assumptions that underpin what we do in the classroom. The development of a clear set of principles regarding effective TEYL practice is important as these help us to make informed judgements about our work and to discriminate between useful resources and teaching practices and those that are not so useful. One of the best ways for teachers to develop principles for TEYL is by engaging in reflective teaching. The ways in which teachers can do this will be discussed in more detail in Chapter 6. Examining some key theoretical perspectives concerning child development and children's language learning processes is also an important way for teachers to develop principles for TEYL practice. In this chapter, we will consider how different theoretical perspectives can help us understand the needs of different groups of young learners and ensure we help children learn languages effectively.

Characteristics of Young Learners

One important place to start in developing a principled understanding of TEYL practice is to consider what is distinctive about children as learners that makes teaching them different from adults. However, this is not as straightforward as it might initially appear to be. This is because as Pinter (2006) notes, the term "young learner" needs to be seen as an umbrella term that covers a wide range of children at different ages. We need to be aware that older and younger children bring different levels of emotional, linguistic, and cognitive maturity to their English language learning classroom.

The well-known child psychologist Jean Piaget (1896–1980) proposed that children go through a number of stages of cognitive development. He argued that children in the early stages of primary schooling, up until the age 7, are in what he called the preoperational stage of development. Children of this age are holistic learners who learn primarily through multisensory experience. They do not yet have the ability for the sort of analytical and abstract thinking that only starts to develop from the age of 8, when they reach the concrete operational stage (for a clear and accessible account of Piaget's stages of development see Pinter, 2011). Piaget's ideas provide useful general guidelines on some important developmental differences between children of different ages, but it is also important to realise that children do not develop at the same rate. Even within groups of children of the same age, we will find children who are at different levels of emotional and cognitive development.

These insights highlight how teachers of young learners need to pay attention to both the linguistic and cognitive demands of the activities and tasks they use with the particular groups of children they work with. Teachers need to make sure that activities and tasks provide the right level of linguistic and cognitive challenge; too little or too much challenge will not be beneficial for learning (Cameron, 2001). We discuss this idea further when we talk about the role of teachers in mediating children's learning later in the chapter.

An awareness of age-related differences can also help us understand what can realistically be achieved with children of different ages. One of the main reasons for the drive to lower the age at which children start learning English as an additional language around the world is the belief that learning at a younger age enables children to learn the language more quickly and improves their chances of long-term success. This belief has its roots in two assumptions. Firstly, it reflects the evident rapid progress that young children are often seen to make in learning English in settings where English is widely spoken outside the classroom, such as in North America or in the United Kingdom. Secondly, it reflects the belief that there is a critical or sensitive period for language learning after which it is much harder for children to achieve full competence in their mother tongue (MT), (Pinter, 2011).

However, these two assumptions are increasingly being called into question. This is partly because there is not enough evidence to prove that a sensitive period applies to additional language learning (and not only the MT). In addition, because in the majority of places where children are learning English they are learning it as a foreign language, they aren't exposed to the English language learning opportunities that enable children who are living in Anglophone countries to make such rapid progress. There is also a lot of research that shows that younger children progress much more slowly than children who start in late childhood (from the age of 9 or 10) when they have greater cognitive maturity (Marinova-Todd, Bradford-Marshall, & Snow, 2000).

These ideas suggest that it is unrealistic to assume that younger children will always make rapid progress in learning English. But, as Johnstone (2009) has argued, this doesn't necessarily mean that an early start isn't worthwhile. Young children bring a great deal of natural curiosity and enthusiasm for learning to the English classroom. They are also typically less anxious and inhibited than older learners. This is therefore an ideal stage to build the positive attitudes and confidence with English that these students will carry forward into their language learning experiences in the later stages of primary schooling and beyond. This is not to say that teachers shouldn't work to develop language skills, but that a key focus should be on activities that are motivating and that these activities match students' interests and knowledge of the world. Because younger children have limited concentration spans, it is also especially important when teaching at this level to make sure that there is plenty of activity variety and that there are many changes of pace during instruction. Young learners can easily get overexcited when engaging in fun activities, too, and teachers need to make sure that as well as activities which "stir," such as active, group, and physical tasks and games, there are others that settle and calm down children, such as listening to stories with the teacher (Read, 1998).

How Do Children Learn Languages?

Teachers of young learners need to develop an understanding of how children learn, and, specifically, of how they learn languages, to help identify ways to support their young learners in the TEYL classroom.

As Cameron (2001) observes, we are only just beginning to undertake research into children's learning of English as a foreign language. However, theoretical perspectives and research into children's development and first language learning can provide us with some useful insights into children's additional language learning processes. We will discuss three of the most important insights here.

Children Are Active Learners

As anyone who spends time around young children will know, children are active learners. They make sense of the world by exploration and experimentation, and by trying to make links and connections between what they experience and what they already know. Piaget referred to this active learning as constructivism. He saw this as involving two processes, assimilation and accommodation (see Pinter, 2011 for a clear treatment of Piaget's concepts of constructivism, assimilation and accommodation). In language learning, assimilation can be illustrated by the tendency for children to over-generalise. For example, young children may learn the word *cat* and then use this to describe all the four-legged animals they encounter. However, through feedback from parents or hearing others use different words to describe different animals, they will gradually come to realise that *cat* only refers to a particular kind of four-legged animal. In other words, they will accommodate this new information into their developing knowledge of the language system.

What does all this mean for what we do in the classroom to support children's learning? First of all, teachers should realise that each child in the young learner classroom is busy making personal sense of the English learning opportunities that the classroom (and possibly their out-of-class world) provides them with. This means that children will focus on different ideas in our lessons and that they will progress at different rates. We need to provide materials and activities that are engaging and supportive of the different needs of the young learners we work with. In addition, because it is not possible to predict what children will learn from the opportunities we provide them with, it is unrealistic to expect all the young learners in our class to achieve a specific set of learning outcomes at the end of the lesson. Teachers therefore need to make sure they recycle key language points at regular intervals in their language learning programmes.

REFLECTIVE BREAK

Consider a TEYL programme you are familiar with.

- How far do the activities and materials support individual differences in language learning?

- Do the activities and materials assume that children learn at different rates?

- Is there evidence of recycling of key language points?

Children Are Social Learners

While Piaget understood that the environment provides an important stimulus for children's learning, his main focus was on describing the universal processes of sense-making that children go through as they develop. Another prominent developmental psychologist, Vygotsky (1896–1934), argues that the experiences children have are central to what sorts of understandings they can construct (Williams and Burden, 2004). As Cameron (2001) observes, he suggests that because learning takes place in social worlds full of other people, we need to understand children's learning as *socially* constructed. In other words, we need to recognise that children are not only active learners, but they are also social learners.

Vygotsky sees spoken interaction as important to children's active construction of knowledge, as this provides them with an opportunity to try things out, to get feedback on their efforts, and to ask questions to check their understanding (Cameron, 2001). For Vygotsky, the quality of the conversational exchanges that children have with significant people in their worlds, such as parents and teachers, can make a crucial difference to their learning. He maintains that under the right sort of learning conditions and with the right sort of support, children can learn much faster than they can on their own (Cameron, 2001).

Vygotsky argues that we need to create a "space" for learning that is just above children's current level of understanding and capability (Read, 2006). He called this space the Zone of Proximal Development (ZPD). Working in a child's ZPD means helping learners to extend their learning in ways which they would not be able to do without the help of someone with more knowledge and skill (see Read, 2006). There are a number of ways in which teachers can create this kind of learning space in their classrooms to help learners with their immediate developmental needs. The sorts of procedures they can use are not unlike those that parents use to help their children master new skills such as learning to dress themselves or learning to ride a bicycle. These include

- building from what children already know to introduce new ideas,

- embedding new learning in familiar classroom routines and activities,

- using questioning techniques and activities to help children notice new learning points,

- showing children how to complete a task, and

- suggesting alternative ways of doing things.

Because young learners in any one class have different support needs, it can be challenging to create a learning environment that addresses all of these, but there are certain teaching strategies which help with this. It is important to use materials and resources that provide a rich stimulus for new learning for all, such as stories or songs. Teachers can then employ activities to work with these materials and resources that provide a structured learning space to meet the different development levels of the young learners they work with. These activities can be carefully staged to target minimal outcomes that most learners can easily achieve, and plenty of extension tasks for those who are able to go beyond these.

REFLECTIVE BREAK

What sorts of materials can teachers use to create a rich and stimulating encounter with language for the young learners they work with?

Young learner teachers need to observe and assess children's efforts to acquire English to help them work out how and when to carefully adjust the support they offer. Too much support will not create the important space for new learning that is needed to help students move forward with English language learning. Similarly, if we try to use activities that are beyond their ZPD, young learners may well end up confused and fail to develop the confidence and feeling of achievement they need to be successful.

REFLECTIVE BREAK

What sorts of things can a teacher do to track the developing needs of individual learners in the young learner class?

Children Are Naturally Meaning Orientated

Research into how children acquire their first language provides some useful pointers to how we should approach language work with young learners of English as an additional language. Research shows that young children first concentrate on those units of language they hear which are most immediately meaningful to them (Cameron, 2001). They first pick up on single words (such as *Daddy*) or meaningful chunks of language (such as *bye bye*). They then start to join words together to form two- or three-word utterances such as *Daddy book*, and then move to notice the ways in which structural units, word order, and tense can help them refine their message so it is better understood. They start to develop an awareness of how their communicative intention can be made more precise (such as *This is Daddy's book* or *Daddy, give me the book*). Over time, they also start to develop an understanding of the relationships that hold between meaningful units of language, such as between *food* and *sandwich*, or between *apple* and *cake*.

The basis for this early language learning is listening to and producing spoken messages. Although children will have plenty of exposure to literacy events from a young age, such as through reading stories with their parents, they do not typically start a process of learning to decode written texts until they reach school and have already built a sizable vocabulary. Another important finding is that, contrary to what is often assumed to be the case, the process of developing proficiency in a first language is not nearing completion until children reach 11 years of age, and this is in spite of their being fully immersed in their MT (Marinova-Todd, Bradford-Marshall, & Snow, 2000).

REFLECTIVE BREAK

Do you think it is important to concentrate more on developing young learners' vocabulary or on introducing grammatical patterns?

The findings above are useful for TEYL teachers as they can help raise awareness of the lexical foundations of early language learning. They suggest that with both younger and older children who are beginning to learn English, teachers should first concentrate efforts on helping children build a solid vocabulary. Teachers also need to provide plenty of opportunities for children to hear and interact in

English in the TEYL classroom to help them with this. Finally, as well as being aware of children's cognitive and emotional maturity, teachers need to consider the stage of development children have reached in their first language in setting expectations and selecting activities for the young learners they work with. With younger children, who do not yet have strongly developed analytical skills, explicit teaching of grammar is likely to be confusing, but including opportunities to help children notice the way this helps fine-tune meaning is useful. With older children, teachers can capitalise on their more developed first language system and their ability to think in more abstract terms about language.

3

From Principles to Practice: Understanding Task-Based Learning

The previous chapter outlined the ways in which children learn, and suggested different approaches to teaching that would support their development. In years gone by, much young learner teaching was a watered-down version of adult teaching methodology, and favoured traditional teacher-fronted lessons. In some parts of the world, this is still the case. This chapter advocates a move away from this methodology, and focuses on topic and task-based learning as the best way of engaging young learners in meaningful learning. Bourke (2006) sums up the situation:

> *Language teaching should relate to the child's world. Children live in a world of fantasy and make believe, a world of dragons and monsters, talking animals and alien beings. In their world there are no tenses, nouns or adjectives . . . . it follows that when we plan a syllabus for young learners, we should make it experientially appropriate. (p. 280)*

Topics and Themes as the Focus for Learning

Many course books for young learners follow a topic-based syllabus, and these topics must be chosen so that they not only provide interest and motivation for children, but also act as the vehicle for language learning. In other words, the topics must be selected so that they are able to provide the necessary conditions and motivating experiences for language learning, as well as generating a range of language structures and functions. Emery (2010) describes the choice of topics for young learners as "challenging" because so many factors are at work. Certain topics are universally popular: for example, food, pets, zoo animals, holidays and travel to foreign countries, historical topics such as Ancient Egypt, science topics such as dinosaurs or the life cycle of a frog or butterfly. However, some topics appear to have universal appeal on the surface, but deeper examination shows they may not actually help learning. For instance, the topic of "clothes" in a course book published for sale internationally may show clothing not worn in a particular country, and children will be expected to learn vocabulary which might have no use for them outside of their classroom.

Cameron (2001) suggests that topic-based teaching can go further than the course book, and teachers can adopt a "theme-based approach" where they are free to select a theme of their choice that will be the basis for the learning over "one or two lessons in a week, or for several weeks in a term, to supplement other work" (p. 184). This would seem to be a good solution to using a course book which the teacher feels is not completely appropriate for children's learning in his or her particular context. However, deviating from the course book while also adhering to the syllabus can be very demanding for teachers.

Theme-based teaching can also be extremely demanding on teachers in terms of planning and implementation: Teachers are required to have knowledge of a wide range of task and activity types which can cater to children of all abilities in a class, making sure that all are engaged and that they do not spend too long on cognitively less-demanding tasks, such as drawing pictures (Cameron, 2001). Teachers will also need to have a certain degree of subject knowledge of the themes they have chosen. If the teacher is a nonnative speaker and the whole lesson is to be conducted in English, this in itself will bring additional pressures for the teacher. As Cameron says, "the potential of theme-based teaching to provide realistic and motivating uses of the language with meaning and purpose for children is clear; the realisation of that potential requires . . . . high levels of knowledge and expertise from teachers" (p. 182).

Tasks and Activities as the Vehicle for Learning

As Emery (2010) says, a topic on its own is not of much use; it is what is done with it that matters—so, careful planning of the tasks, activities, and language that will accompany each topic is important. Traditional course books in the past tended to focus more on linguistic exercises, such as gap-fill or grammar transformations, where there was a right or wrong answer and the linguistic outcome was the extent of the task. These were easy for the teacher to correct, but did not encourage much language learning as there were no cognitive, emotional or inter-actional demands inherent in the exercises. They were also incredibly boring for learners. Hence the recent move toward task- and activity-based learning.

Authors tend to describe tasks and activities in different ways. However, all agree that a task is not restricted just to language but should also contain a finite product as its goal. Often activities given to young learners have very few language learning benefits, but contain social and emotional learning dimensions. These aspects of learning are equally as important for a child as language learning objectives. In this book, therefore, we propose to distinguish between tasks and activities in the following way:

- *Tasks* have clear-cut language-based outcomes that are measurable. Tasks may also involve cognitive demands of the learner. A task has finite boundaries and clearly defined start and completion points.

- *Activities* may also involve language practice and development, but this is not the main focus of what children are asked to do. Activities seek to develop children's social, cognitive, and emotional skills.

As children get older, their linguistic and cognitive needs change, and tasks become more appropriate than activities for learning. Figure 1 shows the gradual swing away from activities for younger young learners toward tasks for older young learners.

For younger learners, most of the things they will do in the classroom can be classified as activities, such as painting, drawing, listening to a story, or sorting plastic animals into families, but as learners get older these will gradually be replaced with tasks that have clear language practice and language learning benefits.

Preparation is the key to good task achievement. Learners should be familiar with the language to be used—a task is not the place to introduce a large amount of new language, although a few new words could be taught and used for the first time. The teacher and the learners must be familiar with the stages of the task and the goal: what is needed for successful completion. Teachers must be familiar with the specific demands of each task and how the class is likely to respond to these, including any potentially problematic areas. They must also take into account the degree of support that learners need for successful task completion, and any external factors likely to impact the task's success: noise; disruptive behaviour; excitability of the class; and time factors such as lesson length, necessity of moving furniture, and cleanup time.

Teachers must also be familiar with the specific demands of each type of task: Cameron (2001) divides these into cognitive- and language-based demands. Language-based demands she describes as "related to using the foreign language and to uses of mother tongue in connection with learning the foreign language," while cognitive

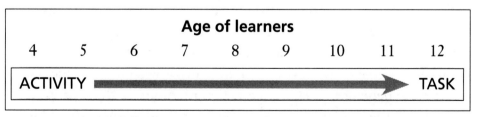

Figure 1. Move from activity-based learning to task-based learning with age

demands are "related to concepts and to understanding of the world and other people" (p. 24). In addition, there will be specific task demands: understanding what is required by the task and what successful completion will entail. It is important that teachers are thoroughly familiar with the demands of each task they set for learners so that they are able to provide the support necessary for the task to be carried out successfully.

Balancing the demands of a task and the amount of support necessary is an important consideration related to the ZPD. If the demands of a task are too high, learners will not be able to complete it in the way expected and, as a result, learning will be compromised. A more dangerous scenario, as Cameron (2001) points out, is that learners may appear to have completed the task, and the teacher may think that they have, but they may not actually have understood or learned from it. It is therefore very important that tasks are closely matched with the age, language level, and cognitive development level of the learners they are intended for. This in itself can pose problems with younger learners who are often at different levels of maturity even though they may be in the same class.

Potential Problems With Task-Based Learning for Young Learners

Carless (2002) raises some potential problems with implementing task-based learning with young learners. The problems outlined here occur most frequently with very large classes; small classes are more manageable, and learners will get more help from the teacher if they need it.

The first issue is noise and indiscipline arising from tasks. In certain circumstances, teachers may find it difficult to achieve a balance between children's involvement in communicative tasks and keeping noise under control, particularly with large classes and when working with learners who are not accustomed to group work or communicative language teaching. According to Carless (2001), this imbalance is most likely to occur when learners are not clear what they have to do, when the task is too easy or too difficult, or when certain types of task are too demanding. He suggests that to minimise these problems, the task must be explained clearly to learners, and learners should be familiar with what is expected of them. In group work tasks, it could be helpful to appoint a leader in each group who is responsible for maintaining discipline and keeping noise levels down.

The second issue that Carless (2001) raises is use of the MT when working on the task. This issue is particularly evident when children are put into groups to work on a specific task: It is much easier for them to complete the task in their MT rather than trying to work in a foreign language. If the class is large and there are many groups, it may be difficult for the teacher to monitor their use of language effectively.

REFLECTIVE BREAK

- Should teachers allow children to use the MT during tasks?

- If so, how much and in what circumstances?

- How can teachers promote the use of English while children are working on tasks?

The third issue Carless (2001) raises is that certain tasks, for instance group work or drama, may involve some pupils in a great deal of speaking or writing practice while others have a relatively small role to play. This will inevitably lead to boredom and frustration on the part of those in minor roles, and will not give them the language practice opportunities that others are getting. It is important therefore that teachers choose only tasks that will afford each group member an equal opportunity to participate, and try to vary the type of tasks so that learners get used to the idea of task progression: working independently on a task one day, working in pairs the following day, and perhaps finally working in a group the third day. By varying the types of tasks that are used, a teacher can make sure that learners are given the maximum opportunity to practice the language as well as cater to different learning styles.

4

Implementing
Task-Based Learning

The previous chapter focused on the topic and on task-based learning in TEYL, and the criteria for selection of tasks to aid learning. This chapter builds on these ideas and suggests some practical ways that teachers can incorporate language-related tasks and activities into their teaching.

Tasks for young learners fall into four main categories:

1. **Board-based tasks.** These are particularly useful for large classes or for teaching contexts where there are few resources and a lack of funding for buying books or other materials. The teacher writes and draws a template on the board, and students either copy it into their books and fill it out individually (or in pairs), or it can be used as a whole-class speaking activity. The grid-matrix is an economical way of extracting the maximum amount of language practice from a single diagram on the board (see Figure 2 for an example of a grid matrix). The template can be used to generate numerous different sentences by cross-referencing the top bar and the left hand column. Typically, these tasks involve use of the four skills plus vocabulary and grammar. They are good for developing all-around language skills.

2. **Paper-based tasks.** These materials can be used either in class or as self-study tasks, for individual or pair work. Paper-based materials lend themselves to integrated skills, and with younger learners, "Read and Do" type tasks such as making a mask or growing bean sprouts.

Can he . . . ?	Swim	Fly	Run	Hop	Climb trees
Does he eat . . . ?	carrots	meat	fish	insects	leaves

Figure 2. Grid Matrix for Eliciting Information About Animals and Teaching Grammar

3. **"Listen and Do" type tasks.** These tasks can involve watching a video, listening to the teacher read a story, or listening to an audio text, and a range of follow-up tasks. They present the teacher with probably the most creative medium of all for developing integrated language learning skills. Chapter 5 suggests some creative methods of developing postreading tasks.

4. **Drama and role-play.** The prompts for these can be printed texts, a story read by the teacher, a video, or an event described by the teacher and developed in class. For example, *My best ever birthday* or, a personal favourite, *A mishap in the restaurant*. Chapter 5 discusses the use of whole-class and small-group drama, which can be used as a postreading activity.

Language learning tasks and materials have to be carefully graded according to age and cognitive abilities, as well as learners' age and language level. This may be seen as a tall order by some, but most teachers are able to accurately match tasks to their classes after they have taught them for a few weeks. Not all learners of a similar age will be able to cope with the same tasks and materials, and as such, this book will not try to suggest an age or grade level for each.

REFLECTIVE BREAK

Can you think of ways in which the same materials might be used with different ages of learners, to create different types of task?

There are three stages involved in setting up and carrying out tasks with young learners, according to Cameron (2001): initial preparation, the core activity, and the follow-up task. The initial preparation stage will focus on introducing the topic, brainstorming any key vocabulary, practicing the grammar to be used, discussing ideas, and so on. During the core activity stage, learners will use oral language in a highly controlled situation. The final stage, the follow-up task, is a less-structured part of the lesson, where learners may work individually, in pairs or groups, and get to practice using the language. A series of lessons illustrating these stages, based around the DVD *The Snowman* by Raymond Briggs (2004) is given on page 36.

The model is similar to Harmer's (2007) Engage, Study, Activate model for teaching older learners. During the activation stage, Harmer says that learners "are encouraged to use all and/or any of the language they know" and that "communication tasks are designed to activate the students' language knowledge" (p. 67). According to Harmer, any meaning-focused activity where language is not restricted will automatically activate language. As such, we can see that this final stage of a task will be the most creative, and will generate the greatest variety of language. By heightening interest in the task, this stage will serve to increase motivation in learning the language: a very important factor when teaching young learners.

REFLECTIVE BREAK

- What kind of tasks do you currently use with your classes?

- How would you categorise them, according the criteria listed above?

- Can you think of ways of extending these tasks so that learners' language knowledge is maximally activated?

Stories provide a stimulating starting point for language work, and, according to Cameron (2001), "if a story appeals to children, they will want to hear it again and again" (p. 175). However, it is not necessary for the story to be read each time; videos provide an equally useful starting point for language tasks. Watching the video will serve as the initial preparation for the task, and, immediately after this, the teacher should ask the class questions related to summary, vocabulary, character evaluation and judgement, story outcomes, and so on. This will help to consolidate the events of the story in learners' minds, and is particularly useful for those who might not have understood all the events while watching. It is important that everyone has a good grasp of the story events before proceeding to the language-related tasks.

The appendix shows a sample lesson plan based on a weekly teaching schedule of six 50-minute lessons, showing how tasks can be integrated with other skills, after watching the video *The Snowman* by Raymond Briggs (2004).

5

Literacy Development and Literacy-Related Tasks

Stages of Reading and Spelling Development

Literacy development in alphabetic languages is thought to develop in a series of stages, and various models of stage development have been proposed (see Ellis, 1997, for a brief overview). In this book, we have chosen to focus on Frith's (1985) model, which indicates that children move through three distinct stages of reading and spelling development, and at each stage either one or the other acts as the pacemaker for the next stage. She terms the stages (1) logographic, (2) alphabetic, and (3) orthographic. A knowledge of theories of development is useful for teachers as the stages can be linked with different types of tasks and teaching methods.

The Logographic Stage

According to Frith (1985), in the logographic stage, children recognise words as wholes by salient shapes within them. They may recognise tall letters and tailed letters, and some rounded letters. However, at this early stage they do not associate letters with sounds and so all words have to be read and stored visually. Ellis (1997) mentions that there is some disagreement over whether the logographic stage occurs only in reading, or whether it can also account for early spelling development. Anecdotal evidence from parents and teachers suggests that there may in fact be a logographic stage of spelling development. Typical spellings at this stage may contain all the letters of a word, but these might be written in the wrong order. This is because the child has memorised all the letters but can't remember the order they come in and, as they haven't yet entered the alphabetic stage, have no knowledge of letter-sound relationships.

The Alphabetic Stage

The logographic stage is very short-lived, for, almost as soon as children have begun to memorise word shapes, they are usually introduced to letters and sounds through phonics teaching and then enter the alphabetic stage. Frith (1985) describes this stage as having three parts: an early, a middle, and a late stage. In this stage, children learn to decode words, reading them aloud letter-by-letter as an aid to pronunciation and thus word recognition (accessing meaning via the lexicon). Alphabetic spelling develops after alphabetic reading, and children begin to realise that sound can be encoded through spellings. Early spelling errors may not appear very phonetic, for example LFT for elephant, but later alphabetic spellings are much more pronounceable: ELFUNT or ELEFANT.

The Orthographic Stage

It is still somewhat unclear how a child moves from alphabetic decoding to the orthographic stage. Frith (1985) believes that this transition occurs through considerable reading practice. However, what is important here is that extensive reading, and lots of practice, is necessary for a child to become a proficient reader and speller. In the orthographic stage, a reader recognises words visually, but this stage differs from the earlier logographic stage in that by this time a reader is equipped with the knowledge of letter-sound relationships, spelling rules, and patterns. This knowledge helps them to recognise words quickly and effectively, and extensive reading practice at this level will ultimately lead to proficient spelling.

Teaching to Support Stages of Literacy Development

So how do these stages of literacy development translate into teaching methods and pedagogic tasks? Logographic reading is dependent on rote memorisation of word shapes, so it is important that children are introduced to books with a restricted vocabulary of high frequency words. The aim is to develop sight word reading of a small range of words, so frequent repetition of the key words is important. A common practice is to use Big Books supported by flashcards at this early stage. These are large size books (with large print, which can be seen by children at the back of the class) containing a simple story, supported by interesting pictures that can be used by the teacher to draw attention to the story and subsequently the words in it. Some Big Books utilise rhyming language, for example:

The children say,

"Pick up that paper!

Pick up that tin!

Rubbish goes in the rubbish bin." (Cowley, n.d.)

Care has to be taken when using books with rhyming language, as this can lead to low frequency words being used to make up the rhyme:

Now every year in Africa

They hold the jungle dance,

Where every single animal

Turns up to skip and prance. (Andreae & Parker-Rees, 1999)

Dance may be a high-frequency word, but *prance* is not. This choice of word may be acceptable to use with native speaking children, but we have to question whether there is any point in teaching such a word to foreign language learners who may never encounter it again. Therefore, when selecting Big Books for use with the class, it is very important that a teacher assesses the language and whether it is appropriate.

Reading aloud is important for children in the early stages of learning to read as it helps to consolidate letter-sound knowledge, and will indicate to the teacher which children have good word-attack skills (decoding and reading by analogy—this will be described later) and which children need further work. Big Books can be utilised in three ways:

- Teacher reads aloud and holds book up to show children the words and pictures, children listen and look at pictures.

- Book is propped up on a small easel at front of the class, teacher points to words with a wooden stick and all children read the story in unison.
- Individual children may be asked to read a page.

As with all books, whether Big Books or longer texts for extensive reading, culture plays a major role in determining whether a child will find the reading interesting or not. Unfortunately, in many countries where English is taught as a foreign language, there is a shortage of children's books written in English for that particular culture. In such cases, teachers will have to rely on books written for EFL learners in other countries, or for native speaking children. The lack of relevant culture will make the story harder to understand, and therefore necessitate more input from the teacher to try to make it comprehensible and at the same time enjoyable. One solution may be for teachers to make their own Big Books. These can be designed from scratch, making up a simple story and (if you are good at art!) illustrating it with big, brightly coloured pictures. However, not all teachers have such skills, so another method is to use a popular children's story: from the Internet, a small reader, or a book of collected stories. The story can be used exactly as in its original form, or it can be modified to incorporate some cultural elements. For instance, the story *The Enormous Crocodile* (1980) by Roald Dahl could be adapted so that it is set in the children's own country, and locally found animals substituted for the jungle animals in the original story. Reference could be made to the local environment: plants, landscape, types of trees found, speech patterns. If the class is keen on artwork, students could draw the pictures to illustrate the story themselves. The teacher can then bind the book and use it to teach reading with this class and subsequent classes.

Sound Awareness and Phonics Teaching

Phonics teaching dominates at the alphabetic stage. There is a wide range of phonics videos available for purchase, and some can be downloaded for free from the Internet. The most important feature here is that the videos should focus on introducing a few high-frequency words only at the beginning, supported by repetition of the letters and sounds that make them up. Phonics teaching is a required component of English language teaching in many countries of the world, as learning to read in alphabetic languages is dependent upon the ability to decode words. This is a skill that readers will rely on all their lives: When encountering a new word, they will have to read it letter-by-letter as an aid to pronunciation.

At this stage, it is important for children to learn that sounds (phonemes) are represented by letters, and that some sounds are represented by more than one letter. In early readings, simple digraphs such as the sound *sh* represented in *shop* can be learned. Children should begin by learning the sounds represented in simple words such as *cat*, *man*, *book*, and *bird*. Children should also be introduced to onsets and rimes in words as this will help them when they encounter words they have not seen before. The onset is the initial phoneme or phoneme cluster, sometimes represented by a single grapheme as in **b**aby, but can also be a digraph or trigraph in more complex spellings, for example, **sch**ool. Teachers can then introduce the skill of reading by analogy: Children can be taught to recognise rimes in words such as *house*, and by substituting a new onset, can read *mouse*.

Care has to be taken not to overdo phonics teaching, or it can become very boring for children. The best practice is to teach it in short bursts of no more than 10 to 15 minutes at a time, using a variety of different techniques such as showing a video, or getting children to read aloud or carry out physical movements in association with letters.

REFLECTIVE BREAK

- Does your MT have an alphabetic writing system?

- How are children taught to read in their first language in your country?

- Do you think this method has parallels to the teaching of early reading in English?

- What challenges do you think children in your country would be faced with when learning to read in English?

Phonemic awareness of the language has been found to be the single most important factor in determining later reading skill in English (Bradley & Bryant, 1983). As such, it is important that teachers give children practice in distinguishing the various sounds of the language. Graham and Kelly (2000) suggest that children might be taken on a "sound walk," where they are asked to focus on different sounds they hear in the environment while walking. These sounds may "vary from bird song to gurgling radiator pipes" (p. 86) and can be done in the classroom if it is not possible to go outside. In this way, children are sensitised to sounds and discriminating between them. Phoneme discrimination tasks using popular children's rhymes can also be used. Graham and Kelly (2000, p. 86) suggest this could be turned into a game in which a rhyming word has been substituted, for example "Hickory, dickory dock; the mouse ran up the watch" and children have to find the rhyming substitution.

Extensive Reading in the Classroom

Once children have built up a small sight word reading vocabulary and can decode and read by analogy, the teacher should quickly move on to extensive reading. At this stage, children are introduced to reading books by themselves, but can also take part in shared reading. Some schools have been lucky enough to convert a classroom into a reading room where teachers can take children for a quiet hour of reading once a week. The reading room usually has no furniture apart from a chair for the teacher and bookcases filled with books; children sit on the floor to read or listen to the teacher reading. It differs from the school library in that the teacher is free to read aloud to the class, and children can read to each other or just sit quietly and read alone. Some teachers have found that it is helpful to keep a record of which books children have read, and so have introduced a book report system where children are asked to write comments about the books they have read, and in this way the teacher is able to keep track of what and how much each child is reading.

It is important that the teacher actively encourages children to read books. At the start, this may involve motivating them through watching a DVD of the book first or having a class discussion about the book. These discussions can begin by looking at the cover and talking about it (What do they think the story will be about? Has anyone in the class read the book or seen it before?) and continue by opening the book and showing the pictures one by one (books with pictures are essential at this early stage). Were their guesses right? What can we predict about the story now? By drawing attention to pictures and brainstorming what the book might be about, the teacher creates interest in the book and children will be more motivated to read it. If class sets of readers are available, then a book can be chosen and parts read in class and other (small, manageable) sections given as reading homework. The teacher should start the next reading lesson by asking questions about the part of the book that was set as reading homework. In this way, children will receive feedback on their reading and will be encouraged to continue with the book. Motivation is paramount in the early stages of reading books in a foreign language.

Teachers can set up class projects based on the characters of a story, and in this way task-based learning can be continued in the reading lesson. For example, characters can be drawn or painted from their descriptions in the book. This might involve reading different parts of the book to gain all the relevant information about physical appearance and clothes. A few lines summarising this information can be written and pasted under the picture. If pictures are large enough, drawn on A3 paper for instance, they can be posted in a line around the classroom walls. This type of approach lends itself particularly well to stories with many characters in them.

Drama as a Post-reading Task

Class readers lend themselves particularly well to drama and role-play activities. If the book has only a few characters, the teacher can divide the class into groups, and groups can decide who will play each part. If the book has many characters, then a whole-class drama can be staged. Whole-class dramas usually require the use of an assembly hall, as desks and chairs in the classroom may get in the way. They also require a great deal of organisation so that each child knows what role he or she is to play and what he or she is expected to do. The teacher will also have to keep discipline and noise under control during these sessions, and children unaccustomed to this approach may see it as an opportunity to let off steam and behave disruptively. Whole-class dramas are encouraged, though, because they provide some of the best opportunities for the class to become engaged with a story. A technique that has been found to be useful in controlling disruptive classes in such circumstances is for the teacher to take on a role in the drama him- or herself. The teacher can then direct the drama in the way he or she wants, without being seen as an authoritarian figure. However, this approach requires experience and confidence on the part of a teacher.

If small groups are set up to enact scenes from the book (or the whole story, depending on the book's length), it is important for the teacher to set a time limit for groups to practice their dramas. When the time is up, the teacher should signal in some way, perhaps by clapping hands, and everyone should sit down quietly in their seats. While the dramas are being practiced, it is important for the teacher to walk round the room, observing each group in turn, listening to dialogue and being on hand to answer any questions or solve any problems which may arise. In this way, the teacher is seen to be involved and supporting the dramas. Without support from the teacher, the children may quickly lose interest in what they are doing.

Finally, groups may be asked to perform their dramas one by one, while the rest of the class watches. Time factors may not permit each group to present every time, so the teacher should make a mental note of which children did not perform this time, and make sure they are given the opportunity to perform first the next time. In this way, everyone gets to participate in the reading, discussion, and drama, and motivation for the story will be heightened.

REFLECTIVE BREAK

This chapter has outlined the benefits of drama as a post-reading task in terms of increasing motivation to read. What do you consider the language learning benefits of small-group dramas for young learners to be?

The Importance
of Reflective Teaching

The purpose of this short book has been to introduce some important ideas to help teachers develop an effective TEYL classroom practice. We have provided some insights into some key theoretical issues in teaching young English learners and examples of how teachers can draw upon these to develop effective classroom practices. We hope this book will be thought-provoking for those teachers already working in this important and growing field. We also hope it will provide some useful pointers for teachers who are interested in making the move from teaching adults to working with young learners or who are embarking on careers in TEYL. In this final chapter, we want to return to the importance of reflective teaching in building a principled understanding of effective TEYL practice, highlighted in Chapter 2.

REFLECTIVE BREAK

What does reflective teaching mean to you?

As Farrell (2013) notes, reflective teaching involves teachers giving more focused attention to the ways they work in class. Being a reflective teacher means taking steps to examine teaching incidents more critically. It involves digging below the surface, maybe to find out why something did not appear to go well or how far something that appeared to go well was actually successful. Being a reflective teacher also means working to deepen an understanding of the relationship between teaching and learning processes.

Reflective teaching is not an optional add-on for TEYL teachers. It is part and parcel of how teachers work to address the diverse needs of children in the young learner classroom. The Reflective Breaks in each chapter of this book provide some possible starting points for engaging in reflective teaching. In terms of how to become a more reflective TEYL teacher, best practices include observing colleagues' classes and inviting other teachers to observe yours, obtaining feedback from learners, and keeping a teaching journal. All of these practices can help teachers identify issues and the ways those issues might be addressed. Innovations can then be put into practice, and the outcomes of this process can be further reflected on.

We believe that there are a number of reasons why undertaking observations of learners in class is an especially important way to promote reflective teaching with young learners. First, young learners are often not able to share their problems or concerns in the way in which older learners can. Observing young learners undertaking activities can help us identify the effectiveness of our teaching strategies and ways in which these strategies may need to be adjusted to ensure we create a nurturing space for growth. It is also a very effective way in which we can develop our understanding of individual children's language learning processes and how to support the development of these. For this reason, many young learner teachers will keep observational records of individual learners to ensure they are aware of, and can work to support, their changing needs. This is achieved by consciously noticing how a particular child performs during the course of a single lesson or over a series of lessons and making notes on what is observed. Teachers often find this a very valuable way to identify ways to improve their teaching as well as to provide concrete information to share with parents so they can also help support their child's English language learning at home.

Finally, as Rich (2014) notes, as TEYL continues to spread across the globe it is both impossible and inappropriate to try to be prescriptive about how teachers should practice TEYL. TEYL practice needs to be context-sensitive (Bax, 1997), and developed by teachers at a local level to reflect their own teaching conditions and the particular needs of the young learners they work with. Reflective teaching is therefore central to identifying how far and in what ways the ideas we have presented in this book are workable for TEYL teachers in the many different and varied teaching settings where they work.

References

Andreae, G., & Parker-Rees, G. (1999). *Giraffes can't dance*. London, England: Orchard.

Bax, S. (1997). Roles for a teacher educator in context-sensitive language teacher education. *ELT Journal, 51*(3), 232–241.

Bourke, J. (2006). Designing a topic-based syllabus for young learners. *ELT Journal, 60*(3), 279–286.

Bradley, L., & Bryant, P. (1983). Categorising sounds and learning to read: A causal connection. *Nature, 301*, 419–421.

Briggs, R. (2004) *The snowman*. DVD. Los Angeles: Universal Studios.

Cameron, L. (2001). *Teaching languages to young learners*. Cambridge, United Kingdom: Cambridge University Press.

Carless, D. (2002). Implementing task-based learning with young learners. *ELT Journal, 56*(4).

Cowley, J. (n.d.). *The litterbug*. Brunei: Curriculum Development Department, Ministry of Education.

Dahl, R. (1980). *The enormous crocodile*. London, England: Puffin Books.

Ellis, N. (1997). Interactions in the development of reading and spelling: Stages, strategies and exchange of knowledge. In C. A. Perfetti, L. Rieben, & M. Fayol (Eds.), *Learning to spell: Research, theory and practice across languages* (pp. 271–294). Mahwah, NJ: Lawrence Erlbaum.

Emery, H. (2010). Developing ELT materials for young learners. In H. P. Widodo & L. Savova (Eds.), *The Lincom guide to materials design in ELT* (pp. 103–116). Munich, Germany: Lincom Europa.

Farrell, T. S. C. (2013). *Reflective teaching*. Alexandria, VA: TESOL International Association.

Frith, U. (1985). Beneath the surface of developmental dyslexia. In K. E. Patterson, J. C. Marshall, & M. Coltheart (Eds.), *Surface dyslexia* (pp. 301–330). London, England: Lawrence Erlbaum.

Graham, J., & Kelly, A. (Eds.). (2000). *Reading under control: Teaching reading in the primary school*. London, England: David Fulton.

Harmer, J. (2007). *The practice of English language teaching*. Harlow, United Kingdom: Longman.

Johnstone, R. (2009). An early start: What are the key conditions for generalized success? In J. Enever, J. Moon, & U. Raman (Eds.), *Young learner English language policy and implementation: International perspectives* (pp. 31–41). Reading, England: Garnet Education.

Marinova-Todd, S. H., Bradford-Marshall, D., & Snow, C. E. (2000). Three misconceptions about age and L2 learning. *TESOL Quarterly, 34*, 9–34.

Pinter, A. (2006). *Teaching young language learners*. Oxford, England: Oxford University Press.

Pinter, A. (2011). *Children learning second languages*. London, England: Palgrave MacMillan.

Read, C. (1998). The challenge of teaching children. *English Teaching Professional, 7*, 8–9.

Read, C. (2006). Scaffolding children's talk and learning. Talk given at British Council 4th ELT conference: *Current trends and future directions in ELT*. Berlin, Germany, 17th–18th February 2006 (available at: http://www .carolread.com/articles/s%20talk%20and%20learning.pdf).

Rich, S. (2014). The added value of international perspectives on teaching English to young learners. In S. Rich (Ed.), *International perspectives on teaching English to young learners* (pp. 191–200). London, England: Palgrave Macmillan.

Williams, M., & Burden, R. (2004). *Psychology for Language Teachers*. Cambridge, England: Cambridge University Press (8th Edition)

Wright, A. (2002) *1000 + pictures for teachers to copy*. Harlow, England: Pearson Education.

Appendix

Suggested Lesson Sequence for Integrating Task-Based Learning With Young Learners

Lesson 1: Initial preparation stage

Focus on watching and understanding the video.

What the teacher will do, and the focus of the task	Approximate timing
1. Teacher warms learners up by asking questions about winter, snow, and making a snowman (e.g., *Have you seen snow? What does it feel like? What can you do in the snow? Has anyone made a snowman? How do you make one?*) 2. Teacher writes a few important words on the board (e.g., *snowman, winter, carrot* [for the nose], *hat and scarf, broom, snowball*).	15 minutes
3. Teacher tells learners they are going to watch a video about a young boy named Alex who makes a snowman and flies away into the sky with him. Explain to the class they should try to remember everything that Alex does and where he goes. 4. Play video.	25 minutes
5. Postwatching questioning and evaluation of story: Teacher asks class questions. Focus on evaluative questions (e.g., *How did Alex feel when he met the other snowmen? Which one did you like best? How do you think Alex felt when he saw the snowman melting?*)	10 minutes

Lesson 2: Core activity

Focus on reading and speaking.

What the teacher will do, and the focus of the task	Approximate timing
1. Recap the events of the video. Teacher asks questions to help learners remember.	5 minutes
2. Focus on key verbs used in the story. Teacher writes key verbs from the story on the board, asks learners to mime them, *or* see if children can match the verbs with pictures of the actions. (A good source of pictures is Wright (2002).) 3. Elicit some language from learners; the video has a musical accompaniment only; there is no speech—this makes it an ideal choice for eliciting language. (E.g., *What do you think Alex said to the other snowmen in the sky?*)	15–20 minutes
4. Jigsaw reading task. Reading and ordering events of the story correctly. Various simplified events can be written on cards, in large writing so they can be seen at the back of the class, and children can be given one each. Students must come out to the front of the class and stand in the correct order to make the story accurate. 5. Teacher reads story aloud: Is everyone holding a card in the correct place? Should any children change places? 6. In place of steps 4 and 5, children could be given a written version of the story which differs from the video in some ways (e.g., specific events might have been changed, or positive adjectives changed into negative ones). See if students can identify the differences.	25 minutes

Lesson 3: Core activity

Focus on drawing and writing.

What the teacher will do, and the focus of the task	Approximate timing
1. Teacher tells children they are to choose a scene from the story and draw a picture of it. When the pictures are complete, each student should write a sentence under his or her drawing explaining the events. Teacher must monitor the class continuously to make sure that everyone knows what to do, pictures are well drawn, and sentences are correctly written.	35 minutes
2. Pictures and sentences can be posted around the classroom walls—children can advise the order, based on the sequence they recall occurred in the video.	15 minutes

Lesson 4: Final stage

Drama

What the teacher will do, and the focus of the task	Approximate timing
Acting out the story. In small groups, one scene acted out by each group, so the whole class gets to participate. (See Chapter 5 for more details of how to organise the class into small groups for drama.)	35 minutes for initial group practice, 15 minutes for group presentations

Lesson 5: Final stage

Focus on a longer piece of writing.

What the teacher will do, and the focus of the task	Approximate timing
Writing the story in their own words. A process-writing approach is best here. Final drafts can be displayed on the classroom walls, along with pictures of events in the story and possibly some photos (taken by the teacher) of the drama from Lesson 4.	50 minutes

The English Language Teacher Development Series

Reflective Teaching (Thomas S. C. Farrell)

Teaching Reading (Richard R. Day)

Teaching Listening (Ekaterina Nemtchinova)

Teaching Vocabulary (Michael Lessard-Clouston)

Teaching Speaking (Tasha Bleistein, Melissa K. Smith, and Marilyn Lewis)

Teaching Grammar (William J. Crawford)

Cooperative Learning and Teaching (George M. Jacobs and Harumi Kimura)

Teaching English as an International Language
(Ali Fuad Selvi and Bedrettin Yazan)

English Language Teachers as Program Administrators (Dan J. Tannacito)

Classroom Research for Language Teachers (Tim Stewart)

Teaching Writing (Zuzana Tomaš, Ilka Kostka, and Jennifer A. Mott-Smith)

Teaching Pronunciation (John Murphy)

Content-Based Instruction (Margo DelliCarpini and Orlando B. Alonso)

Language Classroom Assessment (Liying Cheng)

Teaching Digital Literacies (Joel Bloch and Mark J. Wilkinson)

Teaching English for Academic Purposes
(Ilka Kostka and Susan Olmstead-Wang)

Lesson Planning (Nikki Ashcraft)

Motivation in the Language Classroom (Willy A. Renandya)

Classroom Interaction for Language Teachers (Steve Walsh)

Managing the Language Classroom (Phil Quirke)

Teaching Young Learners (Helen Emery and Sarah Rich)

Language Teacher Professional Development (Thomas S.C. Farrell)

Coming Soon:

Materials Development (Steve Mann and Fiona Copland)

www.tesol.org/bookstore